Alisher Navai
And
Abdur Rahman Jami's
wise words

By:
Saidova Mohinur

© Taemeer Publications LLC
Alisher Navai and Abdur Rahman Jami's wise words
by: Saidova Mohinur
Edition: August '2023
Publisher:
Taemeer Publications LLC (Michigan, USA / Hyderabad, India)

© **Taemeer Publications**

Book	:	*Alisher Navai and Abdur Rahman Jami's wise words*
Author	:	Saidova Mohinur Yoqubjon Qizi
Publisher	:	Taemeer Publications
Year	:	'2023
Pages	:	32
Title Design	:	*Taemeer Web Design*

ALISHER NAVAI

1. A stranger cannot be happy in a foreign land, and a friend cannot be kind to him.

A golden cage is filled with a red flower, and a nightingale is as strong as a thorn.

2. On the path of truth, who has taught you a single letter with pain,

You cannot fulfill it with a hundred thousand gold.

3. Language is a tool of speech with so much honor.

If the speech turns out to be inappropriate - it is a disaster of the language.

4. A person who learns what he does not know by asking is a scientist,

A person who is ashamed and did not ask is cruel to himself.

5. Whoever tells a lie to someone, smears his black face with oil.

Even a little lie is a great sin; even a little poison is deadly.

6. He learns little by little and becomes wise.

7. It is necessary to educate a young child from a very young age.

Education helps a person to develop good habits and qualities.

8. It's like someone who learns and doesn't practice, digs a hole and lays eggs.

9. Good manners earn the blessings of the elders for the younger ones.

10. A person who makes happy for the memory of a single-minded depraved,

Let him be prosperous if the Kaaba is destroyed.

11. If you don't care about a person, it's a person who doesn't care about others.

12. It must be that time is the king of thought, Good for good and bad for bad.

13. Sacrifice your head to your father, Donate your body to your mother's head.

The light that turns into day and night is exposed, One is the moon, the other is the sun.

14. Don't breathe a sigh of relief for your homeland, and don't long for a bitter foreigner

15. A happy garden is a flower of the universe, a flower of a better life.

16. If a person bows to the scholars, then bows to the prophet

17. My pain is heavier than mountain , but my body is lighter.

18. It is impossible to stay in this world forever, but it is a great blessing to leave a good name.

19. Man is superior to other animals with his language. His superiority over other people is known through his language. Language is a tool of speech with so much honor. If the speech turns out to be inappropriate - it is a disaster of the language.

20. "How long will you spend your life in pleasure and sleep?" Are you drunk with pride and covering your eyes with a veil of darkness? It is best to illuminate the dark

nights with sincere obedience, with its light where you are going."

21. The deed that the scholar did not do is acceptable, but the grain did not raise the crop.

22. A bad word will come and hit you, and you will sit down and believe.

23. A bird realized that there is no loyalty in the flower.

24. The people of the time are disloyal, how can you be faithful in the time, The people of the time are faithful, but they want to be faithful, they are ignorant.

25. Say the unspeakable word, back off the unspeakable word.

26. Don't tell your friend bad news, even if it's true; If you find fault with someone, don't blame them. Let the enemy deliver the true news and be patient, he will make the conflict of guilt his enemy.

27. Know that you are a fool, you can't save the world.

28. Let's say that your ego has conquered you, but this does not mean that difficulties and hardships have

completely disappeared (if you know that something is difficult, there are more difficulties).

29. If you are in love, forget about the good and bad things. If the past is bad, forget the regrets, if the future is good, forget the arrangement.

30. Good people hold a conversation together.

31. Not educating a capable person is oppression, and educating an incompetent person is a shame. Don't spoil your education and destroy it, don't waste your education on it.

32. In any case, don't make people happy with your charity while you're alive, and don't remember it with prayers after your death.

33. There is a bit of honor in the human race.

34. The breath of the people of pain is like a balm, it softens the hard heart and makes the dry eye cry.

35. Whose work is the science of contentment, know that what is done is the art of contentment.

36. Someone who destroys knowledge, makes himself and the people proud.

37. If he hurts me a hundred times, I will cry a hundred times.

38. What is worse than ignorance?

39. The fast of sustenance will be prosperous for the one who abandons the morning sleep. Someone who is careless and spends the morning in sleep will see these blessings only in his dreams.

40. If, it is not easy to keep your secret for yourself,

It's not easy for someone else to keep it.

41. A scientist should preserve the stem and quantity of his knowledge and not pound the gem into a stone for examination.

42. Whoever tells a lie to someone, smears his black face with oil. Even a little lie is a great sin; even a little poison is deadly.

43. Under the feet of mothers, Ravzai is the paradise of the devil. If you wish, be the soil of your mother's feet.

44. A person with an open face is far from a flaw like hypocrisy... Joy to the people from an open face; from the salty word, honor to the country. Beloved with humanity; pleasing to souls with humanity. Friends and enemies are calmer than him. Such a person will be blessed in his life.

45. If you don't have good manners, you won't have a court, but the manners are better.

46. Someone who is a human being among the people of the world, knows that he believes in him.

47. Don't talk too much about useless words and don't repeat useful words.

48. O Navoi, no matter how entertaining the fun is, manners and modesty are better and nicer.

49. The world is a mess and it's too easy to pay attention to it.

50. If your self-interest is great for the people, know that this self-interest is great for yourself.

51. I have neither love nor lover's lust.

52. Just as a flower is not free from thorns, so a good person is not free from sorrow.

53. Don't be a fool with too much meaning, an animal with too much work.

54. Collect the wealth of knowledge in youth, spend it in old age.

55. "Love is a bright sun, because of it the thorns of sad hearts become flowers." Love is a shining full moon, the night of dark souls is illuminated by it.

56. I have taken good care of you in the past years, and in recent years, I have been good.

57. O Navai, obey fate as it may, because even the sky is powerless before God's will.

58. Think about your body, whatever you want, you want.

59. When a pearl falls into the mud, its value cannot be grasped and it does not remain at its own value. A donkey wears a pearl crown and wears turquoise lips, and no one forgets his poverty.

60. Don't be crippled by shoelessness, take care of the barefoot and give thanks. (Don't complain that I don't have money, but give thanks to those who have no legs)

61. If a craftsman exaggerates his skills, his nature turns to greed. Arguing people in a madrasah enter into a conversation with arrogance. One denies this opinion, the other that. Everyone recognizes his own opinion and only himself.

62. Aysh, Navoi, how heart-warming they are, but manners and modesty please.

63. Everyone's word is a lie, a liar is a scumbag.

64. If you want to learn guidance from someone, but it does not happen to you, do not despair and do not turn away from the intention of enjoying the grace of God.

65. Let him be friend with the agressive people and let him drink and become a hundred thousand bad things.

66. My pain is heavier, my body is lighter.

67. A person has all his morals, and when he dies, he gives a horse a gift. One is generous, the other is kind, it may or may not be human.

68. Do not spare what you have earned by hard work, and do not keep what you have lost by hard work for friends and enemies.

69. It is much better to die a heathen than to be selfish.

70. There are a hundred people who do not have a job, and there is only one person among the number of people.

71. If you say that someone is a human, then he is not a human being.

78. In words, Navoi, whatever you say is not true, True navo is not praise for the song.

79. If the farmer doesn't feed, it's day and night.

80. Be a soul in the body of the people of this age, and be a medicine for their souls.

81. The body of the flower is almost dead and stained with blood.

82. Let your anger be the only thing you can do.

83. Laughter is abundantly abundant.

84. Highness has come to the target of dedication, and time has brought down the one without dedication.

85. If you don't have a horse, you don't have barley.

86. I tasted all the flavors, I couldn't find any juice sweeter than happiness.

87. It's painful to get a dime, but it's better if someone gives it to you.

88. Human beings want perfection, and even pain is desired.

89. Unbelievably rude people are worthless, and the wheels of the family are high.

90. Nature becomes habit, If it is is old, habit becomes nature.

91. Don't look at the poor, look at the one who doesn't look at you.

92. Don't forget it when you say it, don't take it for granted when you don't say it.

93. If you say that you will find a way, it will be lit on fire.

94. A lot means pride in the word

And a lot of food is lust for the administration.

And with words you can save death,

A dead body is alive with words.

95. It's enough to hurt your tongue,

You know, it's a pain in the ass.

96. Say what you say, take back what you don't say.

A true word is honorable, a good word is short.

97. You have a lot of fun.

Don't tend to the vine, tend to the word.

98. Don't say the word until it's cooked in your heart.

And by all means, keep it in mind - don't mention it.

99. Everyone's words are lies,

Don't believe anyone who tells the truth.

100. Don't talk too much

Don't repeat the useful word too much.

101. Don't take the truth as a lie

He can tell the truth, don't taint the language with lies.

102. There will be a harvest under the guidance of the tongue,

A hundred varieties of bad and bad crops.

103. You don't care about language, you don't pay attention to hand.

A man's beauty is wisdom and knowledge.

104. A wise man speaks the truth,

Well, that's not all.

105. Because when you break your heart, your tongue hurts,

The pain of someone who doesn't come is the pain of the soul.

106. If you want glory, say little.

If you want health, eat less.

107. Who makes up a lie,

When the girl says it's true, keep it.

108. When there is so much need,

If you don't tell the truth, don't tell a lie.

109. He learns little by little and becomes wise.

It gathers together and becomes a river.

110. That everyone did their job,

Think together, people.

111. Collect the essence of knowledge in youth,

Spend it in old age.

112. What a fool, who is a scholar?

He didn't know what he did, but he didn't do it.

113. Perfect my profession, my world is home,

It is obligatory for you to be sad before you die.

114. A person without courage is not in the number of the land,

And a body without a soul cannot be called alive.

115. It's good that everyone knows,

Good enough is good enough.

116. If a man sows a thorn, he will find a bitter one.

And if he sows, he will reap.

117. No matter what a person does,

The printed pattern is revealed on the sheet.

118. If you are a man, you are not a man,

His is the sorrow of the people who don't exist.

119. I don't care about a lover,

If I am human, this is it.

120. There is no craft, and one is alone,

He is the only person among the number of people.

121. An individual can't find anything in time,

Who heard the sound of a lonely palm!

122. There was no honor for the family,

But honor has come, modesty and decency.

123. When someone scatters wheat on the ground,

It's not possible.

124. It is bad if someone dies apparently.

Anyway, it still appeared.

125. Sugar melts like white salt,

But one dissolves salt and one dissolves sugar.

126. He is blind to the people,

Love the one who doesn't love you.

127. If you don't protect yourself,

You should file a complaint yourself.

128. Good luck with your work.

Don't waste your time, just a breath.

129. I tasted all the flavors

Unfortunately, I have not found a sweeter juice.

130. The height has come to celebrate the occasion,

Time has humbled the unselfish.

131. Disaster has happened to someone.

But the reward is tougher.

132. Someone's desire to commit,

He has a hangover.

133. Someone is a slave for a foot of soup,

The face needs the look of a pot.

134. This flower is full of frogs.

If there is a strange happiness, take it with kindness.

135. It's the difference between good and bad,

It is a sinking for two ships.

136. If you don't want to hurt someone,

The mind is equal or not.

137. The existence of a saying that does not give glory,

Who became the humiliation of a civilized person.

138. Too little is not good,

It's not too late.

139. A calm mind and a plow without curd,

Please hug someone with gratitude.

140. How many kings can you find,

Shame on the poor.

141. Nature has a habit,

It's old habit, it's nature.

142. Imagination is not the same type.

No two hadiths are the same.

143. Say that my food will not be wasted, eat it.

And if you wish that my dress does not wear out, wear it.

144. People of the world, as you know, enmity is not work.

Let's die for each other, be kind to each other.

145. If the salt dies, it's a man's business,

What is the name of the person who started the work.

146. To whom the work of husbandry is the land,

There are thousands of people who have done the same thing.

147. A man does not say that he is beautiful and beautiful.

He who is proud of himself is not a man.

148. Everyone dreams of falling in love,

It makes the leaf dry, and the small pox leaves.

149. Don't die carelessly

Can you see the wind when you blow out the candle?

150. Whoever dies, wants to run away.

Because it is necessary to avoid evil.

151. Whose do you want to be?
Don't try too hard, I agree.

152. If you call someone a person, you are not a person.
The form is not identical with the verb.

153. If the seed dies to the fruit, so will the skin,
No one is an enemy or a friend.

154. The meaning is clear enough to expose the moment,
If he doesn't see any sin, he is happy.

155. The appropriate language is tyrannical friends
There are many opponents and enemies.

156. How many diseases are there in the court?
No matter how much it hurts, he is a judge.

157. I remember the world's science today,
All the angry people are the master.

158. Don't spend all day and night for little work,
Don't be hasty in politics.

159. With patience, a lot of related work will be opened,
At work, there is a lot of work.

160. How many fruits to scatter is the work of the horn,
He is the one who picks up more stones.

161. At one point, a letter bends down,
The copy has a crooked letter on every page.

162. People who have no manners are worthless,
It is low and the wheel is high.

163. If you are a wise person, you should spend this time well, it is the work of the ignorant

Die hard for the one who didn't grow up and the one who passed.

164. Be a soul in the body of the contemporary people,
Be a medicine for their souls.

165. Don't be angry with the angry people.

Let it be a hundred thousand calamities.

166. I'm sorry for all the damage,

Who eats food on food.

167. Gentle volunteering can be said to be the anchor of a human ship in a sea full of incidents and can be equated to a scale stone that measures the value of humanity. Hilm ethics is a man's precious garment and it is the most durable fabric of all types of clothing. He is said to be a protector against evil desires and a protector against the futile actions of hypocritical hypocrites. As a result of hilm, a person gains the respect of the people; thanks to hilm, favors and blessings reach from elders to children.

168. When adults make fun and laugh at young people, they feel so insignificant and small in their eyes; When young people are joking and lighthearted towards adults, they are shameless and careless in his eyes.

169. The people of this era are like a poppy in the garden, as light as the wind, and the people of Hilm are humiliated as if they have a heavy nature and bad behavior. And they themselves, like a whirlwind, shake the soil into the air and with their light-hearted nature, they seem to reach the blue. To trample the mountain goat - their habits; to blow the particles from the fields into the air - these are virtues. Such people do not hesitate to enter through every door; he knows no other work than to heat the furnace like

grass. Although the wind blows the crown of the tulip, how can it affect the belt of mountain rocks? The grass can burn the grass at the foot of the mountain, but how can it compare to the spark of the sun?

170. Even if it reaches blue, is still light and worthless; a mountain is healthy even if it falls to the ground. Among the grass there are herbs that can be burned; and in the meaning of hilm, there is a red ember like an ember to be attached to a king's crown.

171. Whoever hurts the heart with harsh words, a bitter tongue will pierce him like a poisoned spear. The wound of the spear of the tongue does not end in the heart; it does not heal the wound.

172. If there is a wound of the spear of the tongue in a heart, only a kind word and a sweet tongue are its salve and comfort. A gentle word turns savages into nobles; the sorcerer - reciting a spell with a melody, pulls the snake out of its den.

173. You don't care about language - you don't pay attention to it. An ezma who talks a lot is like a dog that barks at night until dawn. A person with a bad tongue hurts people's hearts and brings disaster to himself. The barbaric braying of a fool is the free braying of a donkey. A cheerful person speaks a friendly word with gentleness; Any sadness that may come to your heart will be repelled by his words. There is a possibility of any kind of good in the word, that's why they say; "Breath has a soul..."

174. A person who is ugly, talks nonsense, and has an unpleasant voice is like a frog. Language is also a source of pure spirit that gives happiness; The source of the evil star is the tongue. A man who holds his tongue is a wise man; A man who gives free rein to words is a condescending person. It is better if the language is sweet and pleasant; it is better if the language and the heart are one. Tongue and heart are the best organs in a person. In Boston, the most beautiful flowers are hollyhocks, roses, and basils.

175. Man is superior to other animals with his language. His superiority over other people is known through his language. Language is a tool of speech with so much honor. If the speech turns out to be inappropriate, it is a disaster for the language.

ABDURAHMAN JAMI

1. It is necessary to acquire only useful knowledge, avoid useless virtues and listen only to what is necessary.

2. Generosity is not generosity when it depends on something or demands something in return, even if what is demanded is praise and gratitude.

3. Whoever has the following five things in his hand will be a guarantee of a good life: the first is encouragement, the second is safety, the third is the abundance of sustenance, the fourth is a faithful friend, and the fifth is leisure. Whoever is deprived of these five things, the door to a good life is open to him.

4. To throw a humorous ironic shot at the little ones is to sell the reputation of greatness for nothing and sink into the dust of humiliation.

5. If you are hungry, any kind of food will make you hungry. And when you are sitting with you, your appetite will hate you.

6. Do not leave the door in the early morning without a morsel of food in your mouth, for satiety is the fuel of politeness and deep reflection, and hunger is the midwife of frivolity and foolishness.

7. There is no sweeter person in the world than sincere lovers.

8. If the host exalts himself above all blessings around the table, your liver is better than his bread and your blood is better than his juice.

9. A poet read a silly ghazal,

I said, I wrote without alphabet, that's great.

I said that it would be the highest art,

Not even the words of the poem.

10. Look at the old lion with no teeth left, the lame fox is hurting him.

11. A bad doctor is a disaster for everyone, an example is the plague.

The following are prepared on the basis of Alloma's "Bahoristan".

1. If there was no teacher in the world, Life would not be so beautiful.

2. There is no better friend in the world than a book. He cares for you in sad times. Stay alone with him, he will not hurt you, he will give your soul a hundred pleasures.

3. He who calls craft, he is wise, ignorant people know wealth as power

4. Mother is the highest position.

5. If you are alone, my companion is a book, and the light of the dawn of knowledge is also a book.

6. The one who raises the blade of enmity will almost be from the blade of enmity.

Alisher Navai, also known as Nizām-al-Din Ali-Shir Herawī was a Timurid poet, writer, statesman, linguist, Hanafi Maturidi mystic and painter who was the greatest representative of Chagatai literature.

Nūr ad-Dīn 'Abd ar-Rahmān Jāmī, also known as Mawlanā Nūr al-Dīn 'Abd al-Rahmān or Abd-Al-Rahmān Nur-Al-Din Muhammad Dashti, or simply as Jami or Djāmī and in Turkey as Molla Cami, was a Sunni poet who is known for his achievements as a prolific scholar and writer of mystical Sufi literature.

www.ingramcontent.com/pod-product-compliance
Lightning Source LLC
LaVergne TN
LVHW010422070526
838199LV00064B/5386